Start TO Finish
Second Series

FROM Sea TO Salt

LISA OWINGS

LERNER PUBLICATIONS COMPANY • Minneapolis

Lerner Publications Company
A division of Lerner Publishing Group, Inc.
241 First Avenue North
Minneapolis, MN 55401 USA

For reading levels and more information, look up this title at www.lernerbooks.com.

Library of Congress Cataloging-in-Publication Data

Owings, Lisa, author.
From sea to salt / Lisa Owings.
    pages   cm. — (Start to finish. Second series)
    Includes index.
    ISBN 978–1–4677–6019–5 (lib. bdg. : alk. paper)
    ISBN 978–1–4677–6288–5 (eBook)
    1. Salt industry and trade—Juvenile literature.
    2. Seawater—Juvenile literature. 3. Salt—Juvenile literature.
    TN905.N45 2015
    553.6'32—dc23   2014015101

Manufactured in the United States of America
1 – CG – 12/31/14

TABLE OF Contents

I love **salty** snacks! How is salt made?

Salt comes from the sea.

Most salt on Earth comes from the sea. In some places by the sea, the sun almost always shines. The wind blows gently, and rain rarely falls. These are perfect places for **harvesting** salt.

First, workers pump seawater into ponds.

Workers pump seawater into shallow ponds. As the sun beats down, some of the water **evaporates**. The remaining water gets saltier and saltier. The water becomes **saturated** when it can hold no more salt.

Salt crystals form as the water dries.

The saturated salt water is moved to other ponds. There, more of the water evaporates, and this time, it leaves salt crystals behind. The evaporation process often takes years.

Next, workers harvest the salt.

Workers wait until there is a thick layer of salt crystals. Then they harvest the salt. In some countries, workers rake the salt into piles. In others, trucks scoop up the salt.

Trucks take the salt to a factory.

Trucks carry loads of salt to a factory. The factory makes the salt pure and turns it into a variety of useful products.

Then the salt is washed and dried.

Machines at the factory wash the salt to clean it. They use salt water to wash the salt because the salt would **dissolve** in freshwater. Then other machines dry the salt with hot air.

Next, the salt is sorted.

Machines or workers move the clean salt over a series of screens. Each screen allows only certain sizes of crystals to pass through. The screens sort the salt into large, medium, and small crystals. Each has a different use.

Machines package the salt.

Only the purest salt is used to flavor food. Machines pack this salt into **containers**. Then workers ship the salt to stores.

Finally, the salt is ready for your table.

People have enjoyed salt for thousands of years. Grind, shake, or sprinkle a little on your next meal. Bon appétit!

Glossary

containers: objects, such as bags or boxes, that can hold things

crystals: solid substances with many flat surfaces

dissolve: to mix completely into a liquid

evaporates: changes from a liquid into a gas

harvesting: gathering a resource for use

saturated: holding as much of something as possible

Further Information

Boothroyd, Jennifer. *What Is Taste?* Minneapolis: Lerner Publications, 2010. Are your favorite snacks salty, sweet, or sour? Read this book to find out more about your sense of taste.

How to Make Monster Salt Crystals
http://www.marthastewart.com/1004005/how-make-monster-salt
-crystals#1004005
Ask an adult to help you make your own seriously huge salt crystals!

Morton Salt: Fun Facts
http://www.mortonsalt.com/salt-facts/fun-facts
Take this quiz to test your knowledge and learn something new about salt.

Strom, Laura Layton. *The Rock We Eat: Salt.* New York: Children's Press, 2008. Find out about other ways we get salt, such as mining.

Tomecek, Steve. *Everything Rocks and Minerals.* Washington, DC: National Geographic, 2010. Read this colorful book to learn more about salt and other minerals, plus all kinds of rocks!

Index

Photo Acknowledgments

The images in this book are used with the permission of: © iStockphoto.com/JeryB7, p. 1; © iStockphoto.com/Saturated, p. 3; © Koichi Saito/AmanaimagesRF/Thinkstock, p. 5; © Michael Zegers/Westend61/CORBIS, p. 7; © Carolos Goldin/Latin Stock/CORBIS, p. 9; © PavelSvoboda/Shutterstock.com, p. 11; © iStockphoto.com/Hanis, p. 13; © Brett Gundlock/Bloomberg/Getty Images, p. 15; © John Carey/Getty Images, p. 17; AP Photo/Brian Corn, The Wichita Eagle, p. 19; © iStockphoto.com/IS_Image Source, p. 21.

Front cover: © iStockphoto.com/AnrodPhoto.

Main body text set in Arta Std Book 20/26.
Typeface provided by International Typeface Corp.